THE A.B.C.
of
PIANO PLAYING

An Easy Method for Beginners

by

Boris Berlin

———————

Book Two

Revised Edition
Including Elementary Technic for Beginners

New Illustrations by Lida Koníček

Technical Illustrations by Acorn Technical Art Studio Inc.

ISBN 0-88797-149-0

PREFACE

The A.B.C. of Piano Playing has been prepared to meet the ever-growing demand for a simple, yet progressive beginners' series for children.

The material included in this series has been divided into lessons, thus simplifying the assignment task of the teacher. Since children expect to play the piano right from the beginning, each lesson contains simple tunes which the pupil can play while learning about the keyboard and about notation. The Lessons in Writing correspond to the Lessons in Playing. They will prove invaluable as a "theory aid" in learning the pieces.

As in Book 1 of The A.B.C. of Piano Playing, many of the illustrations found in Book 2 contain elements that relate to the corresponding pieces. Thus, in the 1st Lesson, the clouds suggest the interval of a fourth, as found in measures 3 and 4; in the 2nd Lesson, the stars show the pattern of notes that occurs in the first phrase; in the 6th Lesson, the birds suggest the four-note pattern found at the end of the second phrase; and in the 7th Lesson, the cars, ball, and blocks show the pattern of notes that appears in the first four measures. Musical patterns may also be found in the illustrations for Lessons 8, 9, 10, 11, 12, 13 and 15.

Elementary Technic For Beginners, which includes a number of useful exercises, may be found at the end of this book.

As the A.B.C. of Piano Playing is not meant to be self-instructing, the presentation of its contents is left to the teacher.

FOR REFERENCE
THE KEYBOARD

THE STAFF

G or Treble Clef

Brace

F or Bass Clef

1st leger line above.

5th line
4th space
4th line
3rd space
3rd line
2nd space
2nd line
1st space
1st line

1st leger line below.

MARKS OF EXPRESSION AND OTHER MUSICAL SIGNS

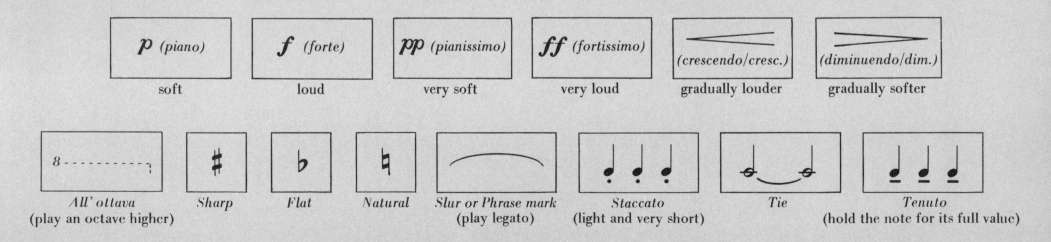

p (piano) — soft

f (forte) — loud

pp (pianissimo) — very soft

ff (fortissimo) — very loud

(crescendo/cresc.) — gradually louder

(diminuendo/dim.) — gradually softer

All' ottava (play an octave higher)

Sharp

Flat

Natural

Slur or Phrase mark (play legato)

Staccato (light and very short)

Tie

Tenuto (hold the note for its full value)

FOR REFERENCE

TIME VALUES

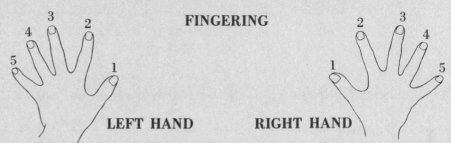

Whole Note (4 beats)
(Tah - ah - ah - ah)

Dotted Half Note (3 beats)
(Tah - ah - ah)

Half Note (2 beats)
(Tah - ah)

Quarter Note (1 beat)
(Tah)

Two Eighth Notes (1/2 beat each, two notes to 1 beat)
(Ti - ti)

NOTES AND RESTS

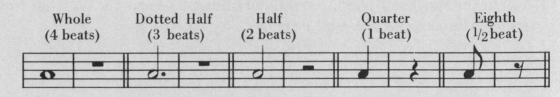

| Whole (4 beats) | Dotted Half (3 beats) | Half (2 beats) | Quarter (1 beat) | Eighth (1/2 beat) |

FINGERING

LEFT HAND   RIGHT HAND

TIME SIGNATURES

The upper figure shows the number of beats to a measure.

$\frac{2}{4}$ $\frac{3}{4}$ $\frac{4}{4}$

The lower figure shows the kind of note to one beat. (The figure 4 represents a quarter note.)

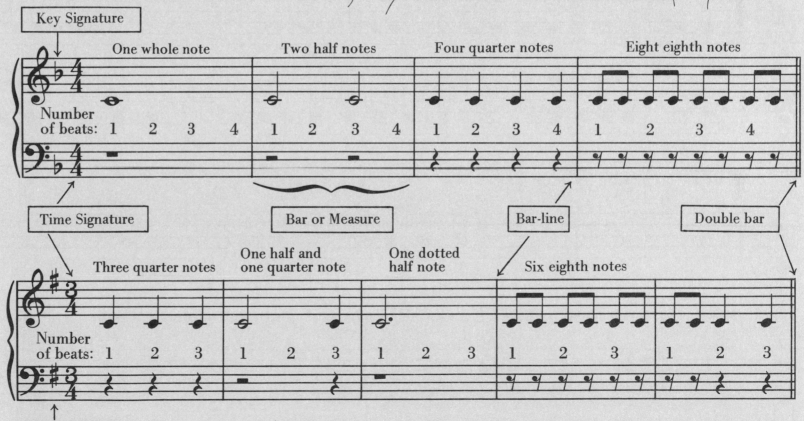

Key Signature

One whole note   Two half notes   Four quarter notes   Eight eighth notes

Number of beats: 1 2 3 4   1 2 3 4   1 2 3 4   1 2 3 4

Time Signature   Bar or Measure   Bar-line   Double bar

Three quarter notes   One half and one quarter note   One dotted half note   Six eighth notes

Number of beats: 1 2 3   1 2 3   1 2 3   1 2 3   1 2 3

Key Signature

1. Fill in the blocks: 1 block for a 1-beat note, 2 blocks for a 2-beat note, 3 blocks for a 3-beat note, 4 blocks for a 4-beat note, and 1/2 block for a 1/2-beat note.

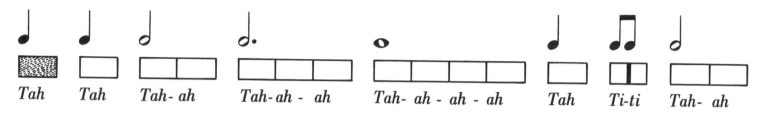

2. Draw bar-lines to divide each of the following into measures.

3. Complete each measure by adding notes.

4. Print the correct letter-name under each note, then circle each pair of notes forming a skip of a THIRD.

Letter-names: G

Date . . . .

Count aloud and clap:

The Country Band

B. B.

Hear the trom-bone sound-ing! Hear the drum-mer pound-ing! Poom, Bah, Poom, Bah!

Now the flu-ter's flut-ing, Red his cheeks with toot-ing, Poom, Bah! Poom.

Remember: ♫ = ♩ (1 count). Notes with the stems joined are two-to-a-count notes. Can you tell the meaning of *f* and of *ff* ?

Second Part
(for duets)

1. Draw bar-lines to divide each of the following into measures, then write the counts for each measure under the staff.

2. Write the meaning of each of the following expression marks.

f _____   *p* _____   *ff* _____   *pp* _____

3. Draw a note of the correct time-value for each letter-name, making sure each measure contains one half note or two quarter notes. Circle each pattern of 3 or 4 notes moving by step or by skip in the same direction (UP, or DOWN).

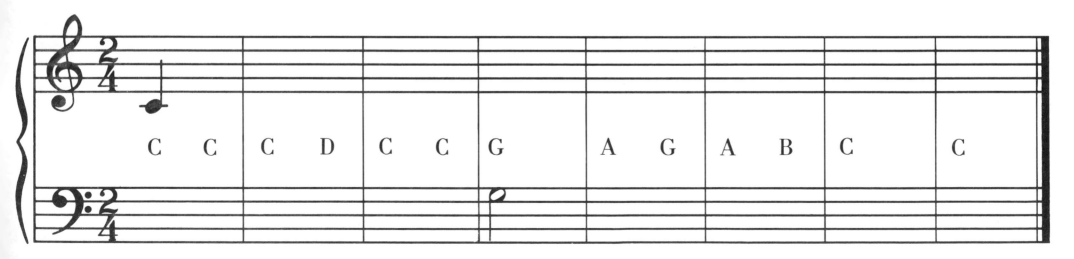

Good King Wenceslas

Remember: The Whole Rest indicates a measure of silence in *any* kind of time.

1. Trace and draw some sharps:
   on the line.

   in the space.

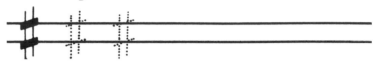

2. Complete each measure by adding notes.

3. Write a time-signature for each measure.

4. Draw an X over each of the F sharps on this picture of the piano keyboard.

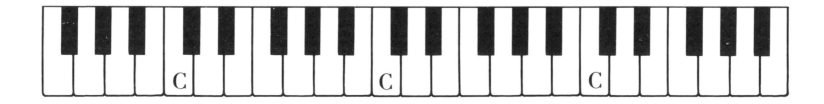

Date . . . .

3rd LESSON

Sharp

Count aloud and clap:

F sharp: Play the black key to the right of the F.

The Birdie

Words by Dinah Lederman

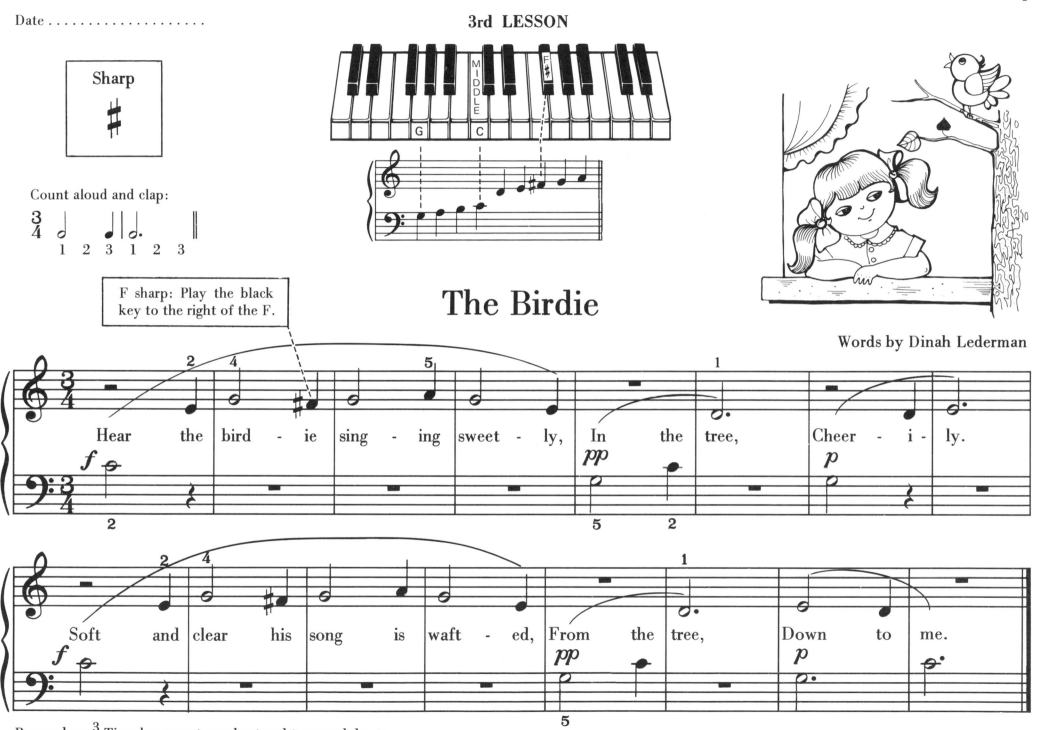

Hear the bird - ie sing - ing sweet - ly, In the tree, Cheer - i - ly.

Soft and clear his song is waft - ed, From the tree, Down to me.

Remember: ¾ Time has one strong beat and two weak beats.
How many phrases can you find in "The Birdie"?

4th LESSON IN WRITING

1. Trace the clef at the beginning of each staff, then draw notes on the staff for the keys marked X. Print the correct letter-name for each note in the space beneath the staves.

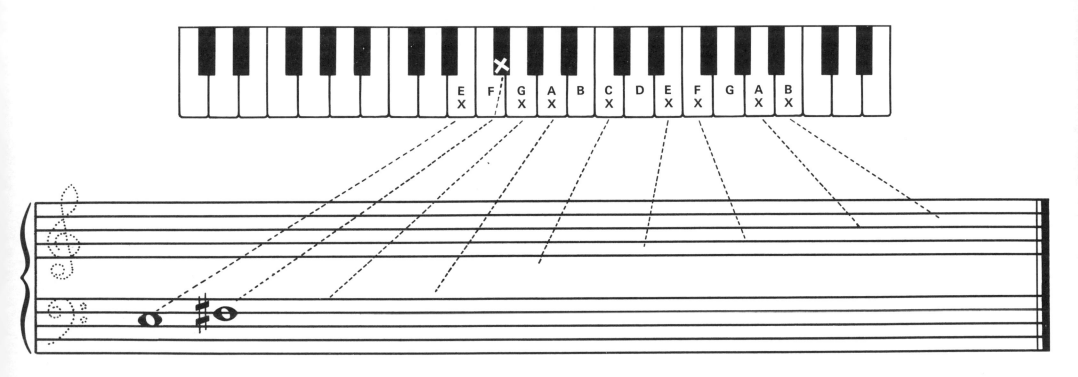

2. Draw bar-lines to divide this tune into measures, then print the correct letter-name under each note.
   Circle the two patterns of 5 notes moving by step in the same direction.

Letter-names:

F♯

Date . . . .

Diminuendo

(gradually softer)

Key Signature

When the SHARP sign (♯) is placed at the beginning of a piece, it becomes the KEY SIGNATURE. In this piece all F's must be sharpened— (played on the *black* key to the right of F).

The Sleigh Ride

B.B.

Let us sing a hap - py tune; Fred, John and Jill,

And we shall be slid - ing soon, _____ Down the hill.

Clap and count the notes in this piece.

1. Complete each measure by adding notes.

2. Print the correct letter-name under each note, then circle each pair of notes forming a skip of a THIRD.

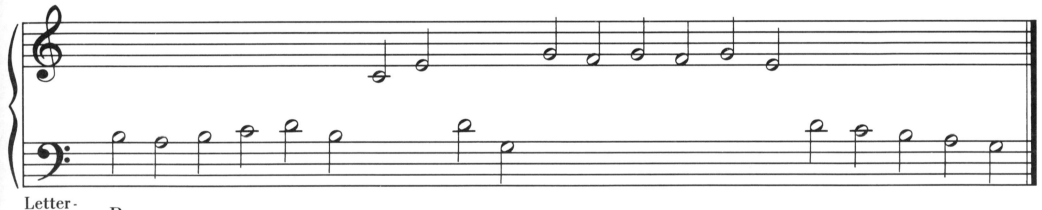

Letter-
names: B

3. For each letter-name, draw a note whose value corresponds to the number of beats shown beneath the staff.
   Draw bar-lines to divide the tune into measures.

Letter-names:	B	A	D	B	D	G	A	F	G	B	D	C	A	F	G
Number of beats:	1	2	1	1/2	1/2	1	2	4	2	1	1/2	1/2	3	1	4

Date . . . .

5th LESSON

Legato

Legato is indicated by a slur or a phrase mark. It means that the notes must be well connected and played smoothly.

Staccato

Staccato is indicated by a dot placed above or below the notehead. It means that the note must be played lightly and very short.

Count aloud and clap:

$\frac{4}{4}$ ♫ ♫ | ♩ ♩ | ♩ ♩ ♩ | ♩ ♩ 𝅗𝅥 ‖
         1 2 3 4 1 2 3 4

The Old Man

Old English Song

Wil - ly, Wil - ly, Will, the old man's com - ing, Wil - ly, Wil - ly, Will, What brings he here?

Wil - ly, Wil - ly, Will, nice su - gar can - dy, Wil - ly, Wil - ly, Will, for you, my lit - tle dear.

The one-beat notes in this piece should be played staccato; the two-beat notes should be held down.

Second Part
(for duets)

1. Trace and draw treble (G) clefs and F sharps.   Trace and draw bass (F) clefs and F sharps.

2. Draw bar-lines to divide this tune into measures, then write the correct letter-name under each note.
   Circle each pattern of 3 notes moving in the same direction (UP, or DOWN).

3. Write the counts under each measure.

Count: 1   2   3   4

Date . . . .

6th LESSON

Tie

A TIE is a curved line joining two notes of the SAME PITCH. It indicates that the second note is held for its full value without being struck.

In a Canoe

B.B.

Can you make up your own words for this tune?

1. Complete each measure by adding notes.

2. Use an X to mark the correct answer. Add arrows in the direction of (a) notes moving UP ; (b) notes moving DOWN .

The notes move:	by step ☐	by step ☐	by step ☐	by step ☐	by step ☐
	by skip ☐	by skip ☐	by skip ☐	by skip ☐	by skip ☐
	up ☐	up ☐	up ☐	up ☐	up ☐
	down ☐	down ☐	down ☐	down ☐	down ☐

3. Draw a sign for each of the following:

soft ☐   loud ☐   gradually louder ☐

Date . . . .

Crescendo

(gradually louder)

Count aloud and clap:

$\frac{2}{4}$ ♩ ♩ | ♩ | ♫ ♫ | ♩ ‖
1   2   1   2   1 2   1   2

Hop, Hop, Hop!

A Folk Tune

f

Hop,   hop,   hop!   Hop, hop, hop, hop, hop!   Hors - ey, you must   gal - lop fast - er,

p

Or you will not | please your mas - ter. | *f* I won't let you stop! | Hop, hop, hop, hop, hop!

Remember: $\frac{2}{4}$ Time has one strong beat and one weak beat.

Which sign means to play staccato?

1. Print the correct letter-name under each note.

Letter-
names: F

2. Add signs to these notes as directed.

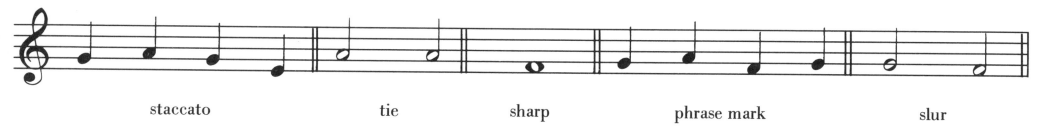

staccato   tie   sharp   phrase mark   slur

3. Draw bar-lines to divide the music into measures, then add arrows in the direction of each of the four patterns.

4. Draw a sign for each of the following:

very soft [ ]   very loud [ ]   gradually softer [ ]

Date . . . .

8th LESSON

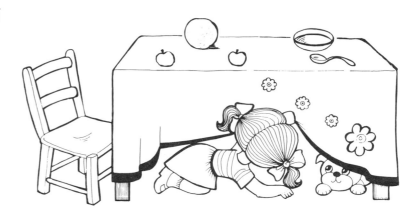

Upbeat

A piece of music sometimes begins with an incomplete measure. The note or notes that appear before the first complete measure are called an UPBEAT, or PICKUP. The following piece begins with an upbeat on the last (third) beat of the incomplete measure. Notice that the time value of the upbeat is taken away from the final measure of the piece.

Oh Where, Oh Where Has My Little Dog Gone?

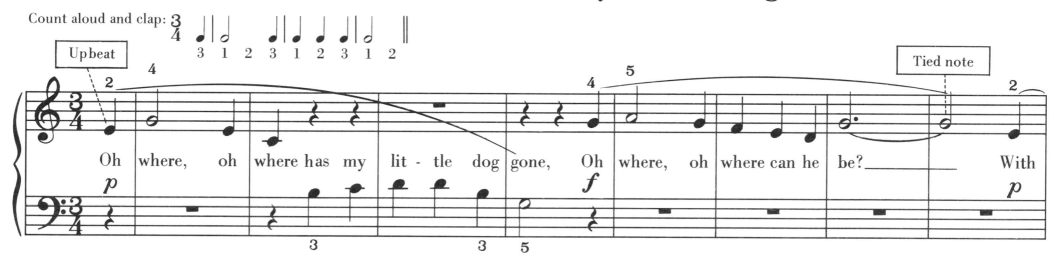

REMEMBER: *p* stands for "*piano*," meaning soft, and *f* stands for "*forte*," meaning loud.

1. Draw notes that correspond to the given rests.

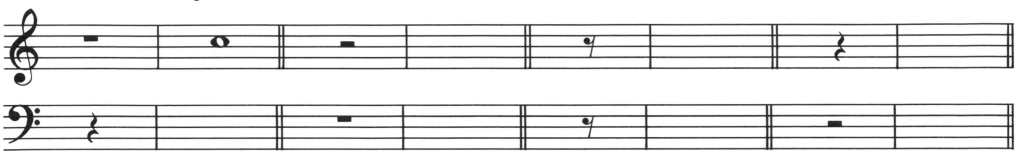

2. Draw signs as directed.

tie 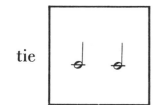   staccato    phrase mark

3. Draw a note for each letter-name, then circle each pair of notes forming a skip of a FIFTH.

E   B   C   G   D   A   E   F   C

4. Print the correct letter-name under each note. (Your answers should spell words.)

Letter-
names: B

Date . . . .

9th LESSON

Count aloud and clap:

Good Night, Ladies!

An Old Song

Good night, la-dies! Good night, la-dies! Good night, la-dies! We're going to leave you now.

Mer-ri-ly we roll a-long, Roll a-long, roll a-long, Mer-ri-ly we roll a-long, On the deep blue sea.

10th LESSON IN WRITING

---

1. Draw notes on the staff for the keys marked X. Print the correct letter-name for each note in the space beneath the staves.

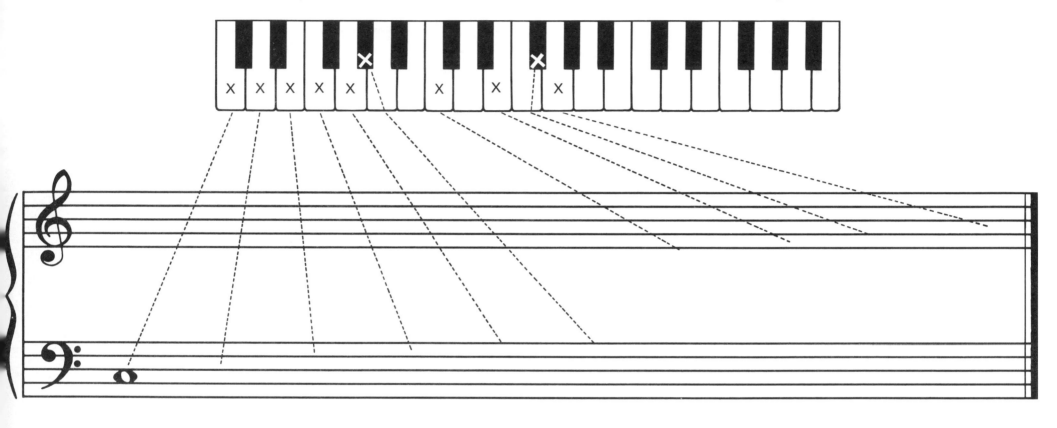

2. Use an X to mark the correct answer.

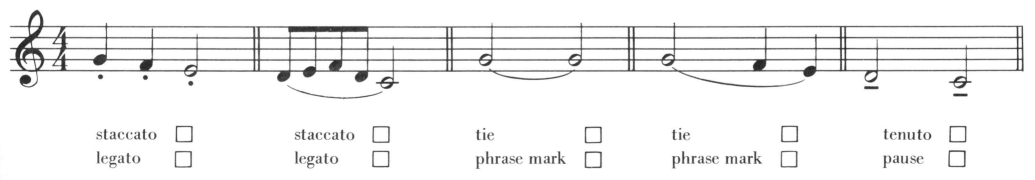

| staccato ☐ | staccato ☐ | tie ☐ | tie ☐ | tenuto ☐ |
| legato ☐ | legato ☐ | phrase mark ☐ | phrase mark ☐ | pause ☐ |

Date . . . .

10th LESSON

Tenuto

Hold the note for its full value.

Count aloud and clap:

MIDDLE
C D E F G   C D E F G
5 4 3 2 1

Buzz, Buzz, Buzz

A Folk Song

Buzz, buzz, buzz,   Bus - y lit - tle bee,   Hon - ey sweet I pray you bring me,

But I hope you will not sting me,   Buzz, buzz, buzz,   Bus - y lit - tle bee.

Note the NEW HAND POSITION in the bass clef.

1. Trace and draw some flats:

on the line.   in the space.

2. Draw a note for each letter-name.

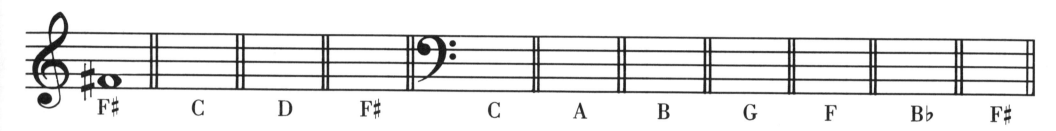

F♯   C   D   F♯   C   A   B   G   F   B♭   F♯

3. Print the correct letter-name under each note, then add a time-signature for each measure.

Draw arrows in the direction of each pattern of notes moving (a) UP ; (b) DOWN ; (c) DOWN and UP .

Letter-names: F

4. Draw rests that correspond to the given notes.

Date . . . .

11th LESSON

Flat

♭

B flat: Play the BLACK KEY
to the *left* of B.

To the Fair

Words by Ruth Fraser Cork

f

Trot, trot, trot, goes the | old gray mare, | Trot, trot, trot, to the | vil - lage fair.

We will sell, We will buy, | Su - gar, cakes, lem - on pie. | Clop, clop, clop! | Clop, clop, clop!

In this lesson there is a NEW NOTE. See how many of these NEW NOTES you can find on this page. Find each one on the piano.

1. Write the meaning of each of the following expression marks.

f _____ p _____ ff _____ pp _____

2. Print the letter-name under each note, then write the counts for each measure in the space between the staves.

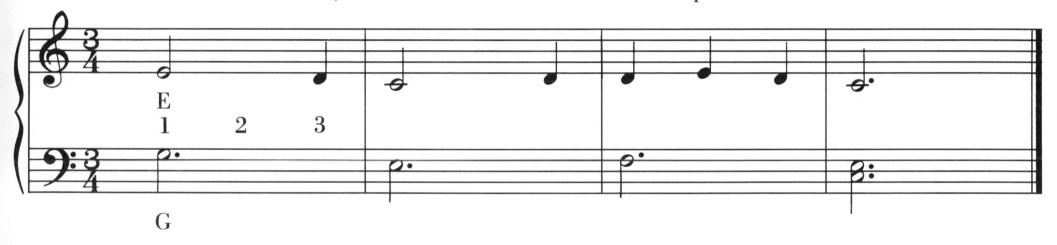

3. Draw bar-lines to divide the following into measures.

Date . . . .

12th LESSON

C - E: a third

Count aloud and clap:

Sleep, My Baby

Words by Ruth Fraser Cork

Sleep, my ba - by, Sleep in your cra - dle.

Close your eyes Till morn - ing is here.

Suggestion: Play each PHRASE three times—first singing the letter-names, then counting the beats, then singing the words.

Second Part (for duets)

R.H.

L.H.

1. Draw a line from each note on the staff to the corresponding key on this picture of the piano keyboard. Then write the correct letter-name under each note.

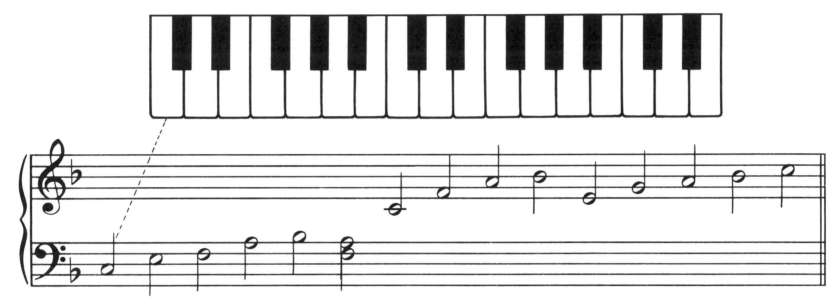

Letter-names:

2. Draw bar-lines to divide this tune into measures.

3. Draw arrows in the direction of each pattern of: (a) notes moving UP ; (b) notes moving DOWN ;

(c) notes moving UP and DOWN ; (d) repeated notes . Circle and name the four skips found in this tune.

Date . . . .

F - A: a third

Key signature

B flat in the key signature means that all B's must be played on the BLACK KEY to the *left* of the white key B. This black key is called B flat.

13th LESSON

The Cuckoo

A Folk Song

Cuck - oo, *p* cuck - oo, wel - come thy song! Win - ter is go - ing,

Soft breez - es blow - ing, Spring-time, *f* spring-time, soon will be here.

What does the upper figure of a time signature mean?
Count aloud and clap the notes in this piece.

1. Draw notes on the staff for the keys marked X, then print the correct letter-name for each note in the space beneath the staves.

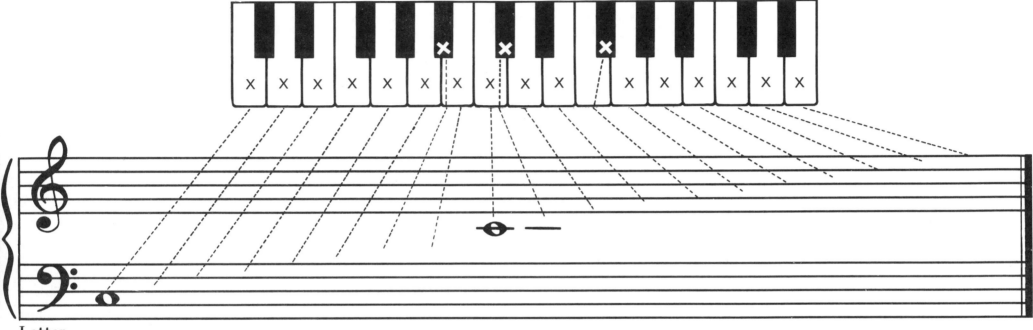

Letter-
names:

2. Write the time-signature and the counts for each of the following measures. Circle each pair of notes forming a skip of a THIRD.

Count: 1   2

3. Make each of the following notes natural.

Date . . . .

14th LESSON

Natural

cancels a
sharp or flat

Count aloud and clap: $\frac{2}{4}$ ♩ ♫ ♫ ♩ ‖
1 2 1 2

We Play Hockey

Words by T. R.

Fast skat - ing, Sticks fly - ing, We play hock - ey! Fast skat - ing, Shoot-ing pucks,

See the goal - ie move. Fast skat - ing, Scor - ing goals, Hock - ey's fun.

C Natural

There is a NEW NOTE in this lesson. What is it?

1. Write the notes that correspond to the given rests.

2. Circle each pair of notes forming a skip of a THIRD, a FOURTH, or a FIFTH.
   Draw arrows in the direction of each pattern of notes moving: (a) UP and DOWN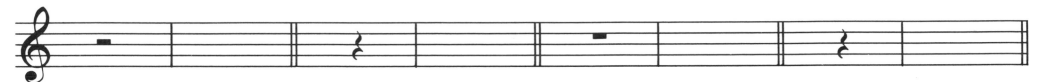; (b) DOWN and UP ;

   (c) UP and DOWN and UP .

3. Draw bar-lines to divide this tune into measures, then print the correct letter-name under each note.

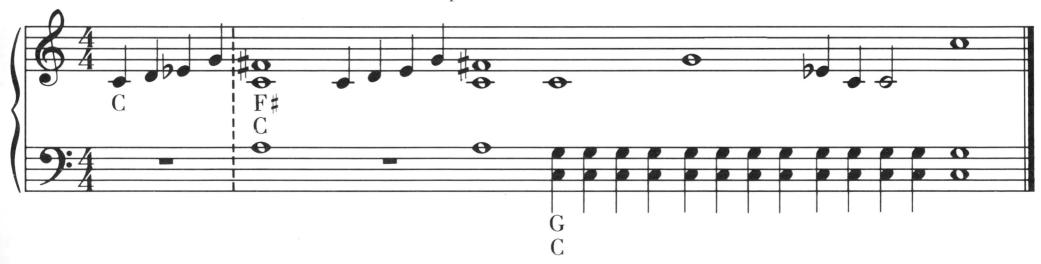

Date . . . .

Indian Days

B. B.

1. Complete each measure by adding rests.

2. Draw bar-lines to divide the following into measures. Print the correct letter-names under the notes, then circle each pair of notes forming a skip.

3. Use an X to mark the correct answer.

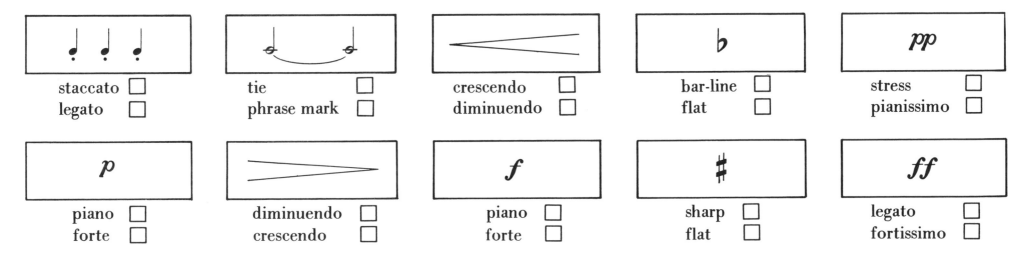

staccato ☐
legato ☐

tie ☐
phrase mark ☐

crescendo ☐
diminuendo ☐

bar-line ☐
flat ☐

stress ☐
pianissimo ☐

piano ☐
forte ☐

diminuendo ☐
crescendo ☐

piano ☐
forte ☐

sharp ☐
flat ☐

legato ☐
fortissimo ☐

O Canada

Majestically

arr. by B. B.

*The ♩. ♪ rhythm can be played by ear.

The Star-Spangled Banner

arr. by B.B.

(Pause)
Hold the note longer than its full value.

*The left hand plays in the Treble staff. The ♩. ♪ and ♩. ♪ rhythms can be played by ear.

ELEMENTARY TECHNIC FOR BEGINNERS

(To build the hand and to develop the player's skill and co-ordination)*

Practise hands separately, one hand after the other.

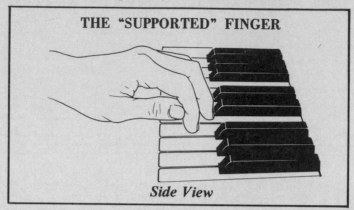

THE "SUPPORTED" FINGER

Side View

Step 1 — FOR LEGATO PLAYING

1. Play any key with the thumb (1st finger).
2. Hold the first key down while playing the following key with the next finger.
3. Release the tied note on count "3".
4. Continue in this way, using one finger after the other.

Example: R.H.

Count: 1 2 3 4   1 2 3 4   1 2 3 4   etc.

L.H.

Count: 1 2 3 4   1 2 3 4   1 2 3 4   etc.

Step 2 — FOR STACCATO PLAYING

1. Support the 2nd finger with the thumb (1st finger), placing its tip against the lower joint (tip) of the second finger.
2. Play each note with the supported finger. Make the sound very short by springing your hand downward and upward from the wrist and letting the key bounce up.

Example: R.H.

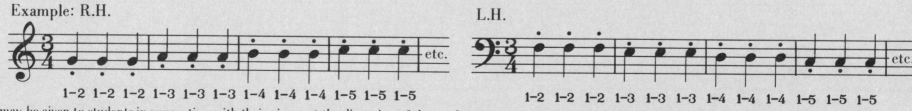

1-2 1-2 1-2 1-3 1-3 1-3 1-4 1-4 1-4 1-5 1-5 1-5

L.H.

1-2 1-2 1-2 1-3 1-3 1-3 1-4 1-4 1-4 1-5 1-5 1-5

*These exercises may be given to students in connection with their pieces, at the discretion of the teacher.

Step 3 FOR SCALES

1. Support the 2nd finger with the thumb as in Step 2. Do this with each hand.

2. Place both hands on the keyboard with the *tips* of fingers 2, 3, 4 and 5 on the correct keys.

3. Play one note after the other *legato*, connecting the two notes as smoothly as possible.

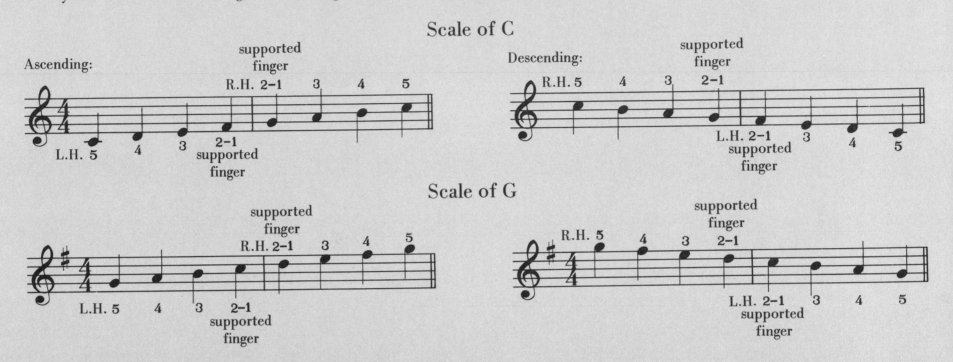

Step 4 COMPLETE SCALES

1. Now try to play complete scales with traditional fingering.

CERTIFICATE

This certifies that

_____

has completed

PART TWO

and is eligible for promotion to

PART THREE

of

The A.B.C. of PIANO PLAYING

_____
Teacher

_____
Date